There has been interest in the awareness for counselors to become leaders and advocates in the community. Underprivileged communities have been in need for counseling advocates for many years (Chang, Hays, & Milliken, 2009). One of the prevailing issues in the community has been domestic violence. Domestic violence has been associated with discrimination and oppression within the African American communities. In has been recognized, in the black community people seek refuge and safety in churches (Brade & Bent-Goodley, 2009).

Spirituality has played a vital part in the African American community for years (Collins & Moore, 2006). The black church is a place of worship and understanding. In the African American community, victims of domestic violence usually seek guidance within their spirituality.

Reading scriptures and attending services helps these individual copes with everyday stressors. Unfortunately, the Black churches lack the skills and sensitivity to handle domestic violence situations (Brade & Bent-Goodley, 2009).

African Americans has been viewed as many things. The American people have created stereotypical views on what and how Blacks act and socialize. There have been mass media coverage and print on negative attributes of the Black American. One of the stereotypical implications that have been around since slavery was buffoon, gullible, and strongly influenced (Roberts, 2009). This was the best indication of this culture. On a bad day they were considered ignorant and loud. Mammy and welfare queen are best associated with this group. The world views are based on living arrangements and survival techniques associated with the conditions of their community.

African Americans beliefs have been stigmatized as superstitious. This idea was presented because of the differences in comparison to European Americans (Roberts, 2009). There has been little effort in understanding African American Culture. In the most part most of the traditions have been lost due to acculturation and forced beliefs during slavery. One of the traditions that is still in practice is Kwanzaa, which is celebrated around the same time as Christmas but is celebrated over the course of days. Each day represent a different theme in Black pride. Jumping the broom is a ritual created in slavery to indicate matrimony. In those days' slaves were not allowed to have a traditional wedding in a church or considered to be in a committed relationship because of the possibilities of being traded. One major historical attribute to African Americans is their experiences in history and the beliefs.

One belief that was circulated in the African American community was the Churches Chicken phenomena. They believe it was owned by the Ku Klux Klan. The reasoning behind this conspiracy was the many chains of restaurants that started to pop up in minority communities. At the time many restaurant chains hesitated and even resisted opening a business in these areas. Due to the mass development of chains in predominantly black communities people started to question its purpose. They believed this organization added extra ingredients to target black people in hope that the product sterilizes males. Blacks also believed that the CIA was responsible for trafficking crack and other drugs into the community to destroy and eliminate African Americans and their environment (Roberts, 2009).

Frederick Douglass documented in his autobiography, *"Narrative of the Life of Frederick Douglass, "I have found that, to make a contented slave, it is necessarily make a thoughtless one. It is necessary to darken his moral and mental vision, and as far as possible, to annihilate his power of reason. He must be able to detect no inconsistencies in slavery; he must be made to feel that slavery is right...."* Considering this selection many people thought the KKK was trying to despise their motives with a stereotypical idea behind all Black people love chicken. Devising a plan to contaminate something that is enjoyed by a specific culture would be the best way to get rid of them.

Even though these beliefs were circulated through the community; it has not stopped Black people from eating at these food chains. Harriet Tubman best described this act as a slave mentality. She said; *"I freed a thousand slaves. I would've freed a thousand more, if they only knew they were slaves."* There is a modern definition; A person conditioned to quietly, and without objection, accept harmful circumstances for themselves as the natural order of things. They're also conditioned to accept their master's view and beliefs, about themselves, and strive to get others, within their group, to accept the master's view.

The beliefs expressed has yet to be proven but is widely discussed and mentioned in the Black community. At the same time people choose to eat at these restaurants anyway. When working with African American people these types of beliefs and traditions should be considered and incorporated in treatment goals and assessments. Some of the things to consider is personal perception, fear of social stigma, traditional coping strategies, support systems, financial issues sense of self, level of resiliency, and psychological development.

Also, counselors should recognize the most ideal way people in this culture cope. In the past they learned to be obedient so that they avoid abuse and displacement from love ones. Currently people in this culture rely on faith, racial pride, spirituality, community connectedness, resources such as public assistance and family. When these components are not considered certain problems could arise in treatment.

A few of the problems of African Americans in seeking good counseling treatment, is the inherent health disparities in the community mental health arena (Das, Olfson, McCurtis, & Weissman, 2006). Das, et al., (2006) cite many reasons for this in their meta-analysis of articles throughout Medline dating from 1966-2004, as well as hand-checked bibliographies to attain more sources "relevant to the evaluation and treatment of African Americans with depression" (Das, et al., pg. 30). These reasons include: clinical presentation differences in somatization, diagnosis stigmas (competing clinical demands of co-morbid general medical problems, physician-patient relationship problems, lack of comprehensive primary care services, under diagnoses, high-risk populations are overlooked, and inadequate management (Das, et al., 2006).

Understandably, this is but only an analysis of African Americans diagnosed with depression. However, the resulting reality is still wholly negative. They state that because African Americans are more likely to seek care in this setting, they are also more likely to need quality care, more so than whites (Das, et al., pg. 31). However, this reality does not exist. The disparities between the recognition of treatment and the treatment itself, seems like a "lost-in-translation" scenario--unable to express what exactly is wrong or the unwillingness of the counselor not being able to detect it from hidden/verbal signs.

Furthermore, reasons for the disparities are disturbingly numerous, including "more likely to be poor, uninsured, or have restrictive insurance policies and to have limited means of transportation to reach health services" (Das, et al., pg. 30). Further complicating equality in treatment is what they deem, the "unsettling irony." They state,

> For emotional distress, African Americans are more likely to seek help from primary care clinicians than from specialty mental health providers. However, in primary care, depression in African Americans is less likely to be detected than it is in whites. (Das, et al., pg. 31)

It must be reiterated that this is simply a study on African Americans seeking treatment for depression. This doesn't consider worse mental illnesses, just depression. Starking is the fact that even though this is the attempt to receive treatment for depression, the reasons for the inability to receive adequate treatment is the same. They claim that most African Americans face many challenges in their day-to-day life, thus "economic factors and illness severity do not fully account for the observed racial differences in the rate and quality of treatment of mental disorders" (Das, et al., pg. 31). They state that the racial disparity can't be justified in any way, but the reasons for it are so numerous that it is probably within the public domain and not necessarily the medical. Thus, I claim that it is the result of the social and not wholly the medical/business model that is in place. The social will always affect the medical/business, since the world is made up of people and without people, there would be no world. Since African Americans have had the worst done to their cultures (through the systematic killing of culture through racism and slavery in the past), it is undeniably and disturbingly sad that even in the community mental health arena, they are still denied the best treatment, because of social dilemmas at work.

Strategies to aid in the counseling of African Americans can be shared with knowledge of their cultural past. Effective counseling strategies are available if the counselor understands the emic and etic ways of counseling (Sue & Sue, 2008). African Americans often have concerns about stigma (from the social aspects) and spirituality (individual), thus, they are less likely to find antidepressant medication acceptable and even tolerate certain classes of psychotropic medications poorly (Das, et al., 2006). A counselor must look at gathering concerted efforts to improve the quality of care for those seeking it, reform health care and health care financing to better accommodate the various issues African Americans face, and gain more awareness in the racial disparities that exist. However, a counselor can't be entirely systemic. Instead, they must "shift from narrow focus to a view of self-in-cultural context," (Frank & Williams, 1996), thus making them more multiculturally aware. Frame & Williams (1996) go on to state that all aspects of African American culture should be focused on, such as: by integrating spirituality in the counseling context, as well as by understanding their use of metaphor, their ideas of social change, their love for music, and celebrating their ideas of their communalistic nature, as many minorities are extremely communal (Frame & Williams, 1996). They continue (1996):

African American culture is rich with

religious and spiritual traditions and practices that largely

have been ignored in traditional approaches to

counseling with this population...the prominence   of the

African American church, the importance of Biblical

themes such as liberation and   freedom, the centrality of

music from indigenous African rhythms to the Negro

Spirituals, to   blues, soul, jazz, and rap are all aspects

of African American spirituality that largely have been

ignored in traditional approaches to counseling with

this population. (Frame & Williams, pg.   16-17).

Constantine, Lewis, Conner, & Sanchez (2000)

continue with this desire for counselors to become

increasingly multiculturally competent in stating that

prayer even yields beneficial uses. Knowledge of this is

necessary, because "prayer as a coping strategy may

reflect, in part, some African Americans' attempts to

minimize the potential stigma associated with using formal mental health services" (Constantine, et al., pg. 31). There is a possible stigma against counselors who are also not religious themselves, such as "clients may be reticent to bring up spiritual or religious issues in the context of traditional therapeutic relationships because they are not willing to present for treatment with counselors who are not explicitly religious" (Constantine, et al., pg. 33). Thus, multicultural competence and awareness are key in counseling strategies for the African American community. Underlying philosophies and therapeutic theories aside, certain techniques of treatment have proven to be effective, such as the Jones Models and Racial/Cultural Identity Models that Sue & Sue (2008) state. Also, Cognitive Behavioral Therapy is an effective form of therapy, one that Das, et al., state in their meta-analysis. However, the term that sticks out to me, most, is having knowledge of a term called, "invisibility." I will

conclude with this statement, which is a huge beckoning

call for counselors to attain multicultural competence and

awareness, in which I believe Franklin (1999) states

correctly in his definition of invisibility, which is,

considered a psychological experience

wherein the person feels that his or personal identity and

ability are undermined by racism in a myriad of

interpersonal circumstances...Awareness of the

dynamic interface between racism, invisibility, and

racial identity development can help the   counseling

process and effectiveness..." (pg. 761)

Techniques are not so much important as the multicultural

awareness that one must first have of the African

American's in general. By being able to transcend between

emic and etic approaches, as well as remaining spiritually

and culturally aware, rapport can be established with much more confidence and dignity. An effective counselor knows there are numerous amounts of facets to African American culture that can be utilized well in a counseling experience to elicit a therapeutic relationship beneficial enough to aid in whatever means they need. I believe that through holism and the gaining more knowledge increases a counselor's ability to be more competent in all arenas, not simply African Americans.

Counselor educator and supervisor can provide advocacy within the African American churches by exercising their service- leadership. Service-leader defined as a leader who has the desire to serve individuals or organizations to promote wellness (Lewis, 2012). As a service leader, the counselor would be providing advocacy counseling. Advocacy counseling would be the best course of action for domestic violence awareness in the Black church. Advocacy counseling defined as counselors who leave their place of work to promote wellness in the community (Hays, Green, Orr, & Flowers, 2007). This form of advocacy falls within the scope of social justice.

Counselor educator and supervisor provide leadership and advocacy through social justice. Social justice is the view that everyone deserves equal opportunity. These include equal job opportunity, equal economics, and equal social rights. Counselor educator and supervisor (CES) applying leadership and advocacy aim to open the door for equal opportunity for those in greater need. In order to facilitate this process, the CES individual most know their professional identity.

Developing a professional identity is very important when working with people in need of services. The counselor must engage with individuals and the community to understand the cultural view of domestic violence. The counselor must possess a strong identity. They must examine their biases and cultural values. Especially when advocating in the religious realm. The counselor does not want to come across as being judgmental or against the church beliefs. This is very important before the counselor go into the community. The counselor would have to understanding that they are not there to advocate for religion but to promote wellness.

Promoting wellness in the community contain the social justice principles along with counselor identity to help assist in structural problems in the community. Providing that counselors know how to create long-term goals of empowering individuals; they use their counseling skills and knowledge to suggest changes to protect the clients in the community.

The counselors should have competency and knowledge of general information regarding the community and the available resources (Hayes et al., 2007). Proper assessment, documentation, and intervention will need to be researched and studied before going out into the community. Reading about the domestic violence statistics in the area is important as well. Counselors should also educate themselves on the safety of the community. Advocacy and leadership in African American communities with high crime rates could be a factor worth thinking about. Planning a safe passageway through the community would be needed to ensure your safety in and out of the community.

In order to effect positive change within the community the counselor must identify the problem.

Making an effort to seek and gain knowledge and awareness of the cultural and situational issues that surround domestic violence in the African American community is important (Williams, Oliver, & Pope, 2008). There is a need for counselors to address domestic violence in the African American churches. Pastors can minimize the problems with domestic violence.

African Americans are reluctant to seek out professional help from community agencies for several reasons. There have been several barriers identified in the African American community such as issues of secrecy, racism, racial stereotyping, and racial loyalty (Brade & Bent-Goodley, 2009). These barriers created a reliance on personal strength, family, and their faith. African American women have relied on their congregation to help them cope with abuse. Yet there have been issues regarding pastors holding offenders responsible for their actions (Collins & Moore, 2006).

A survey conducted of 1,000 victims of domestic violence concluded that one in three received assistance from pastors and clergy and that pastor were unprepared and ineffective with providing adequate counseling when dealing with domestic violence (Collins & Moore, 2006). Collins and Moore (2006) also stated that pastor have misguided African American women by telling them to work harder in their relationships. They stated that women were urged to use prayer for help and in most cases to be more submissive to their partners.

In addition, some pastors' fears to address domestic violence could come from an internal source (Brade & Bent-Goodley, 2009). Pastors may not believe the victims story. In this case, pastor could come off insensitive, untrusting, and manipulative to domestic violence victims. According to Brade and Bent-Goodley, (2009), pastors may not want to talk about or challenge accusation due to their own behaviors. The pastor could be an abuser. Women who are in an abusive relationship with a pastor find it to be harder to seek help because they don't want to run the risk of damaging the reputation of the church.

Pastors and offenders often use scripture to distort and justify domestic disputes (Collins & Moore, 2006). The two most recited scriptures are Ephesians 5:22-28 states that women should be submissive to their husbands and Malachi 2:16 reads, "For I hate divorce". These scriptures and others have been used destructively in the church to condone and keep women in abusive relationships. These practices leave African American women confused about leaving the relationship. The combination of God disapproval and the fear of the offender cause mental issues for the women and children.

In children, it could come out thru aggression and antisocial behavior. Child exposure to violence in the home has estimated to range from 60 to 70% (Hayes et al., 2007). Child exposure to domestic violence have been linked to children continuing the cycle of violence as they get older by being the victim or the abuser (Ireland & Smith, 2009). They may also experience anxiety, sleep disturbances, depression, suicide, and running away (Hayes et al., 2007). Ireland and Smith (2009, argued exposure to violence could teach the child that it is ok to control others and that it is acceptable and normal.

The women suffer from isolation, feeling of hopelessness, indecision, and poor self-confidence (Hayes et al., 2007). In the African American community, women may not recognize the impact of pastoral misguidance. The lack of education in the Black church can result in a continued cycle of control and abuse if not addressed (Collins & Moore, 2006). The counselor educator should focus on these factors to help advocate for support and services within the African American churches.

Counselor educator and supervisor can provide advocacy and leadership to help the African American community and Church by identifying churches that are willing to collaborate with them to address domestic violence. The CES individual could identify the African American community they wish to provide leadership. Letters and phone calls could be sent out to local churches to see if they are interested in pursuing collaboration. Every church may not respond or agree. This should not be deterrence because the response of one church could still make a difference.

After an agreement has been established, the CES person must first educate the congregation on statistics and risk factors of domestic violence (Brade & Bent-Goodley, 2009). Training and preparation need to be implemented within the church. The pastor could create a committee of volunteers who would sit for the training and implement them. The training would consist of identifying signs of abuse, when to notify the police and/ or DCFS, and skill development in addressing domestic violence issues (Brade & Bent-Goodley, 2009). The CES individual could establish a period of times they would go to the church to supply new information and training as needed. Ensure that they stay within their advisory role and employ the ideas and knowledge of the church.

After the training and preparation, the CES individual could help establish a form of early intervention with young males. This workshop would include topics like how to treat partners, anger management, dignity, and equality. This workshop would also teach proper scripture readings and interpretations. Recruitment of older African American males to host workshop would be an ideal part in the development and teachings of young males (Collins & Moore, 2006)

The counselor educator and supervisor could help the church employ a response team. Helping the church create a response to could be viable to promote safety to the individual. Pastors would have to put together a group of people that would be willing to assist women to the local shelter, hospital, and/or police station. The safety of the volunteers and individual would have to be assessed to make sure both parties would not be harmed. In doing so, the individual would have a better sense of safety and alleviate some of the worrying, fear, and hopelessness that they may be experiencing at the time (Collins & Moore,

2006).

In accordance with the response team the counselor educator and supervisor could help the pastor create an emergency response directory. This directory should include but not limited to names and phone numbers of domestic violence shelters, law enforcement, social services, therapist, 24hr emergency hotlines, and professional interventions (Collins & Moore, 2006). These numbers should come in handy just in case the situation becomes too intense and dangerous for the abuser and the congregation.

The counselor educator and supervisor could also assist in networking. Connecting with local businesses, schools and other churches can expand the scope of resources and help. This network could provide additional safety, shelter, food, and spiritual wellness (Hayes et al., 2007). This could also lead to other churches collaborating with the effort to promote domestic violence awareness. Sometimes it takes the observation of one organization to inspire others. The movement could create a ripple effect and soon the whole community would be aware and educated on domestic violence, which could eventually create a positive effect in the community.

Another workshop to establish is pre-marital preparation counseling. The pre-marital counseling could be in form of a workshop or sermon. This would teach the congregation on faith-based practices that utilize good communication skills, moral authority, and conflict resolution (Collins & Moore, 2006). It would promote awareness of violent attitudes and challenges. The CES individual could provide reading materials and guidance that could benefit partners.

Another practice to promote positive community engagement would be to assist the African American church with developing a fundraiser. This fundraiser would consist of gathering items that could assist local shelters. These items would consist of personal care items, nonperishable food, inspirational reading, and clothes. This could become very helpful for those individuals and families who left expediently from the residence to seek safety. In these cases, people usually leave with what they have on at the time. Providing a comfortable and equipped environment would ease some of the fears and stress accompanied with domestic violence experiences.

Counselor educator and supervisor should also educate the pastor and the congregation on mental health concerns and when it necessary to consult professional counseling help. There are different conditions that may accompany victims of domestic violence. Some of the conditions are substance abuse, and depression, posttraumatic stress disorder. These conditions need immediate first aide counseling and pastors need to be educated and informed of the signs, symptoms, and treatment for those conditions (Hayes et al., 2007).

It is important that counselors facilitate community support and individual support. The survivor of domestic violence should also have direct services. Providing direct services to the victim can help aide the church. The CES worker could volunteer services at the church to provide discreet counseling services. Providing services at the church could help the client with confidentiality, safety, and assurance. This could also alleviate shame and fear because the services would be in the church. There would be little effort in transportation.

In the process, counselors could help women recognize the effects of the domestic violence situation. Educate them on the effects it could have on them and their children. The counselor could assess if that client needs further treatment outside of the church. Resources and support will be provided at the time. Clients may not want to ask the pastor for the resources in fear of embarrassment. Having reading material at hand on days volunteering is essential.

This guide examined the role of Counselor Educators and Supervisors in the community and the characteristics in providing leadership and advocacy. This guide discussed the significant of the professional identity of Counseling Educator and Supervisor and how it helps with leadership in social justice. Counselor educators and supervisor play many roles in the African American community. These roles consist of being a clinician, leader, advocate, and advisor. Providing leader and advocacy in the black church could be a challenge. Churches have programmed through religious beliefs, scriptures, and spiritual intuitions from the pastor.

Counseling Educator and Supervisors help effect positive change in the community by advocating for wellness and safety. Promoting awareness in the African American church is one way of promoting change within the community. It gives victims a place of safety and refuge. In African American communities' safety and refuge is usually associated with churches. Collaborating with congregations would have reach people who are not comfortable with traditional counseling interventions.

References

Brade, K. A., & Bent-Goodley, T. (2009). A refuge

for my soul: Examining African American

Clergy's perceptions related to domestic

violence awareness and engagement in faith

community iniatives. *Social Work and*

Christianity, 36, 430-448.Retrieved from

http://proxy.govst.edu:2048/login?url=http://s

earch.ebscohost.com/login.aspx?direct=true&

db=psyh&AN=2009-22002-004&site=ehost-

live

Chang, C. Y., Hays, D. G., & Milliken, T. F.

(2009). Addressing Social Justice Issues in

Supervision: A call for client and Professional

Advocacy. *The Clinical Supervisor*, 28, 20-

35. doi:10.1080/07325220902855144

Collins, W. L., & Moore, S. E. (2006). Theological

and Practice issues regarding domestic

violence: How can the Black Church help

victims? *Social Work & Christianity, 33*, 252-

267. Retrieved from

http://proxy.govst.edu:2048/login?url=http://s

earch.ebscohost.com/login.aspx?direct=true&

db=psyh&AN=2006-21865-002&site=ehost-

live

Dixon, A. L., & Dew, B. J. (2012). Counseling

Practice: Schools, Agencies, and Community.

In C. Y. Chang, C. A. Minton, A. L. Dixon, J.

E. Myers, & T. J. Sweeney, *Professional

Counseling Excellence Through Leadership

and Advocacy* (pp. 207-225). New York:

Routledge.

Hays, D. G., Green, E., Orr, J. J., & Flowers, L.

(2007). Advocacy Counseling for female

Survivors of Partner Abuse: Implications for

Counselor Education. *Counseling Education and Supervision*, 46, 184-198. doi:10.1002/j.1556-6978. 2007.tb00024.x

Ireland, T. O., & Smith, C. A. (2009). Living in Partner-violent Families: Developmental Links to antisocial behavior and relationship violence. *J Youth Adolescent, 38*, 323-339. doi:10.1007/s10964-008-9347-y

Lewis, T. F. (2012). Foundation of Leadeship: Theory, Philosophy, and Research. In C. Y. Chang, C. A. Minton, A. L. Dixon, J. E. Myers, & T. J. Sweeney, *Professional Counseling Excellence through Leadership and Advocacy* (pp. 21-40). New York:

Routledge.

Williams, O. J., Oliver, W., & Pope, M. (2008).

Domestic Violence in the African American

Community. *Journal of Aggression,*

Maltreatment & Trauma, 16, 229-237.

doi:10.1080/10926770801925486

Constantine, M. G., Lewis, E. L., Conner, L. C., & Sanchez, D. (2000). Addressing spiritual and religious issues in counseling african americans: Implications for counselor training and practice. *Counseling & values, 45 (1)*, pgs. 28-39.

Das, A. K., Olfson, M., McCurtis, H. L., & Weissman, M. M. (2006). Depression in african americans: Breaking barriers to detection and treatment. *The journal of family practice, 55 (1)*, pgs. 30-39.

Frame, M. W. & Williams, C. B. (1996). Counseling african americans: Integrating spirituality in therapy. *Counseling & values, 41 (1)*, pgs. 16-29.

Franklin, A. J. (1999). Invisibility syndrome and racial identity development in psychotherapy and counseling African American men. *The counseling psychologist, 27 (6)*, pgs. 761-793.

Fuertes, J. N., Mueller, L. N., Chauhan, R. V., Walker, J. A., & Ladany, N. (2002). An investigation of european american therapists' approach to counseling african american clients. *The counseling psychologist, 30 (5)*, pgs. 763-788.

Sue, D. W. & Sue, D. (2008). *Counseling the culturally diverse - Theory and practice* (5th ed.). Hoboken, NJ: John Wiley & Sons.

www.ingramcontent.com/pod-product-compliance
Lightning Source LLC
Chambersburg PA
CBHW020610300526
45785CB00022B/3026